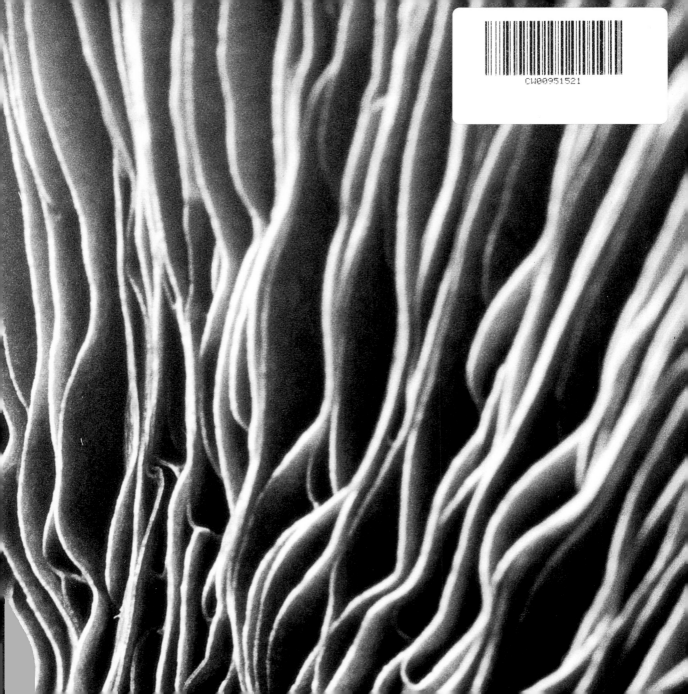

# mushrooms

# mushrooms

## Alastair Hendy

photography by Simon Walton

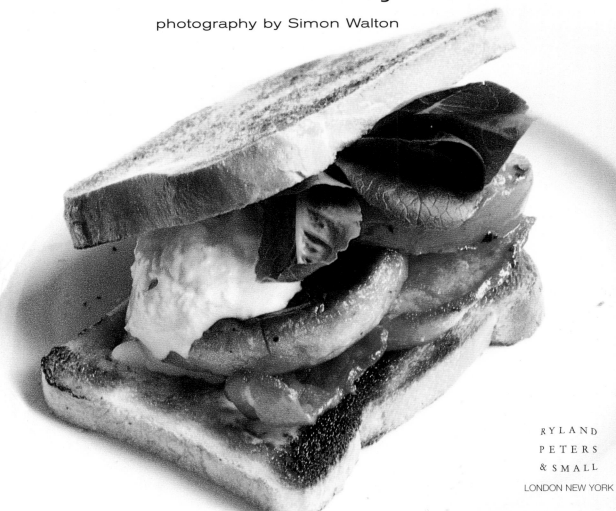

RYLAND
PETERS
& SMALL

LONDON NEW YORK

First published in Great Britain in 2002
by Ryland Peters & Small
Kirkman House, 12–14 Whitfield Street,
London W1T 2RP
www.rylandpeters.com

10 9 8 7 6 5 4 3 2 1

Printed in China

ISBN 1 84172 338 X

A catalogue record for this book is available from the British Library.

## DEDICATION

To Antonio and Priscilla

## THANKS TO

Simon Walton for excellent clicking
Elsa for sampling and forking
Kate and Becca for doing and loving
Egg for beautiful bowling
Halcyon Herbs for growing.

**Senior Designer** Steve Painter
**Designer** Sarah Walden
**Commissioning Editor** Elsa Petersen-Schepelern
**Editor** Kathy Steer
**Production** Deborah Wehner
**Art Director** Gabriella Le Grazie
**Publishing Director** Alison Starling

**Food Stylist** Alastair Hendy
**Cooking Assistants** Kate Habershon, Becca Hetherston
**Prop Stylist** Alastair Hendy

### Notes

Cooking and eating wrongly identified mushrooms can be fatal. If in
doubt, don't. Neither the author nor the publishers can accept any
legal responsibility or liability for any errors, omissions or mistaken
identification of fungus species that may be made.

All spoon measurements are level.

All eggs are medium, unless otherwise specified. Uncooked or partly
cooked eggs should not be served to the very young, the very old,
those with compromised immune systems, or to pregnant women.

Specialist Asian ingredients are available in larger supermarkets and
Asian stores.

## contents

# introduction

I grew up on mushrooms on toast. We'd collect tiny field mushrooms – the common-or-garden sort – from the soft green edges of a nearby golf course. This had to be done early before the caps had time to break their gill veils, unfurl their flesh-pink ribs and flatten out. We'd then throw them straight into a frying pan – back home or on an open fire in the wood – and let them squeak and bounce in a foam of hot butter, then eat them fast, with slabs of buttered toast to act as juice collectors. Fantastic.

Field mushrooms are my love. From chubby pearl buttons to fully fledged, large, open mushrooms. And there are the brown-capped chestnuts, large portobello mushrooms with flaky caps and sweet nutty flavour, and yellow-topped horse mushrooms which taste of aniseed and, like shiitake, turn wonderfully slippery when cooked in simmered dishes.

And mushrooms these days go far beyond the field varieties. There are weird ones, mostly available to the experienced fungi gatherer, with taste and textural nuances that are uniquely delicious. Others are not and can be fatal. So don't touch, if you don't know. Go to the shops instead. These are picked by people who know their mushrooms, and many wild varieties are now farmed.

Recipes too often call for a particular wild mushroom – and more than likely one that you can't, for love or money, get in your neck of the woods. I don't insist on a particular variety in these recipes. I find any mixture will do for most things and if you're stuck with the regular cultivated sort, inject a little aromatherapy by adding a few rehydrated slices of dried porcini or a dash of truffle oil – the highly affordable answer to the totally unaffordable white truffle – and enjoy the musk of the deep forest this way.

So how do I prepare them? Mushrooms are fast food: you have to do little to them or with them to make a very good supper. Most cultivated mushrooms need the briefest wipe with a soft cloth or a pastry brush, to release any peaty particles that may still be clinging. If using truly wild ones, they'll contain unwanted parts of the forest floor, or could be clogged or stuck with dirt around their stumps, so will need more thorough brushing or wiping down with a damp cloth. Washing mushrooms in water – as

controversial as this may sound – is not a sin. It's untrue that deterioration begins in minutes. A quick plunge into cold water won't harm them, especially if they're going to end up in a braise or soup.

Things like fresh porcini and the larger fungi pulled from the wild will often need to be peeled around their bases (and watch out for any wrigglers that have set up home in their stems). Jettison anything that looks unwell and pasty about the gills: mushy watery bits mean the mushroom is on its last legs – it's rotting, and its texture will be unpleasant. All that then remains is to nip off any woody bits of stem – trimming down shiitake stems, as they can be particularly chewy, but leaving things like chanterelles intact – and you're ready to cook.

One last note: many mushrooms are strictly seasonal and some still steadfastly refuse to be farmed and will not conform (or perform) to man's production methods. Scarcity makes things special and keeps a feeling of seasonality around these ingredients. The mushroom kingdom is one of the last bastions of wildness. Thank God.

**toasts, soups and salads**

We all know and love this one so well. But I had to include it, just in case anyone had forgotten just how good it is – no set of mushroom recipes would be complete without it.

## peppered button mushrooms on buttery toast

Working in batches if necessary, put the butter into a large frying pan, melt over medium heat, add the mushrooms and fry until well browned, about 3 minutes. Don't lower the heat too much, otherwise the mushrooms will release all their delicious juices back into the pan and start to boil, rather than fry. Season with salt and plenty of black pepper.

Toast the bread until golden brown and spread generously with butter. Put the toast onto 4 heated plates and pile the mushrooms on top. Spoon any remaining pan juices over the top, sprinkle with extra pepper and serve.

4 tablespoons unsalted butter, plus extra for spreading

500 g button mushrooms

4 thick slices white bread

sea salt and freshly ground black pepper

**serves 4**

9

## portobello panini
## with prosciutto and artichokes

Cooking is all about spontaneity and choosing what looks good when you're out shopping. A jar of fat little *carciofi* (Italian baby artichokes), plump portobello mushrooms, some fine slices of Parma ham and a pot of basil ended up in my basket – perfect for this lunchtime panini.

8 portobello mushrooms

3 tablespoons olive oil,
plus extra for brushing

2 garlic cloves, crushed

1 tablespoon fresh marjoram
leaves (optional)

350 g jar baby artichoke hearts
in olive oil, drained

a large square of focaccia
or 2 semi-baked baguettes

8 thin slices prosciutto, such as
Parma ham

a handful of basil or salad leaves

sea salt and freshly ground
black pepper

**serves 4**

Heat a ridged stove-top grill pan. Brush the mushrooms liberally all over with olive oil, then rub them with salt and pepper, add to the pan and cook until they're just tender and branded with heavy black grill marks – about 2 minutes on each side.

Spread the garlic and the marjoram, if using, on top of the mushrooms on their first cooked sides, flip over and grill again for a further 20 seconds or so, to cook the garlic.

Meanwhile, put the artichokes into a food processor with a little salt and pepper and blend to a purée.

If using focaccia, cut the slab horizontally in half through its thickness, then each half in half again, producing 4 thin slices. If using baguettes, slice in half lengthways. Spread one side of each slice with the artichoke paste, then sit 2 mushrooms on each, stem side down. Add the ham and some leaves, then top with the remaining bread. Lightly brush both sides of each sandwich with oil and put onto the preheated grill pan. Weigh them down with a heavy frying pan or saucepan on top to flatten them out. Pan-grill for about 45 seconds, then carefully turn them over and grill the other side – watch they don't burn. Serve hot.

4 large portobello mushrooms

2–4 tablespoons olive oil

2 beefsteak tomatoes, each cut into 4 thick slices

4 burger buns, pita breads, flatbreads or 8 slices crusty bread

unsalted butter, for spreading (optional)

1/2 red onion, finely sliced into rings

rocket or other salad leaves

sea salt and freshly ground black pepper

**rosemary aïoli**

1 fat garlic clove, chopped

1/2 teaspoon sea salt

2 teaspoons finely chopped rosemary leaves

1/2 tablespoon olive oil

6 tablespoons mayonnaise

freshly squeezed lemon juice, to taste

**serves 4**

Portobello mushrooms are meaty and very succulent – they seem to hold their sweet juices well. For vegetarians, they're the perfect meat-free burger, but if you're an omnivore, add a little crispy bacon or soft ruffles of Parma ham. Or, if like your burger closer to the fast-food variety, add a slice of soft mild Cheddar and a sliced gherkin.

# portobello burger
## with tomatoes and rosemary aïoli

To make the aïoli, mash the garlic with the salt to form a paste. Mash in the chopped rosemary, then mix in the oil, beat in the mayonnaise and add lemon juice to taste.

To make the burgers, heat a heavy frying pan. Brush the mushrooms liberally all over with olive oil, then rub them with salt and pepper. Add to the pan and cook over high heat until tender (you may need to add more oil). Remove from the pan and keep the mushrooms warm. Add the tomato slices to the hot pan and sear briefly, about 30 seconds on each side.

To assemble, split the buns and spread with butter, if using. Add the onion rings, mushrooms, tomatoes, aïoli and salad leaves, close the buns, then serve.

Hon shimeji mushrooms grow in clumps like families – tiny babies sprout at the feet of the dads. To keep the silkiness of their satin-like flesh, they need a short flying visit to a hot frying pan. If they are unavailable, use sliced shiitakes or regular mushrooms. For the photograph, I used golden beetroot rather than the regular purple kind: when cooked, I think they look like nectarines. Add the hot beetroot to the dressing, so they absorb the flavours as they cool.

# baby mushroom salad
## with golden beetroot and ginger

Put the sugar, balsamic and cider vinegar into a bowl and stir until the sugar dissolves. Take the grated ginger in your hand and squeeze the juice into the bowl. Discard the gratings. Add 2 tablespoons of the olive oil and the lemon juice and beat well. Add the onion.

Cut the beetroot into small wedges, add to the bowl, sprinkle with salt and pepper and set aside for at least 30 minutes.

Just before serving, put the remaining 1 tablespoon olive oil into a frying pan, heat well, add the mushrooms and garlic and cook over high heat until seared but not soft. Add to the bowl and toss in the dressing.

Divide the vegetables and dressing between 4 bowls and serve.

**Variation** For something more substantial, mix the salad with shredded carrot and oak leaf lettuce, top with a spoonful of soft goats' cheese and sprinkle with pomegranate seeds.

1 tablespoon caster sugar

1 tablespoon balsamic vinegar

1 tablespoon cider vinegar

5 cm fresh ginger, peeled and finely grated

3 tablespoons extra virgin olive oil

freshly squeezed juice of ½ lemon

1 small red onion, halved and sliced lengthways

4 beetroot, cooked and peeled

a bundle of small mushrooms, such as Japanese hon shimeji or shiitake

1 garlic clove, finely chopped

sea salt and freshly ground black pepper

**serves 4**

To make a good panzanella, mix all the ingredients together (minus croutons and cheese) a good hour or so before you need it. This allows enough time for the mushrooms and other vegetables to give up their juices to the dressing. If you like anchovies, add them too.

# grilled mushroom panzanella

¼ loaf white country bread

300–350 ml extra virgin olive oil

2 fat garlic cloves

1 large mild red chilli, deseeded and coarsely chopped

3 tablespoons red wine vinegar

a pinch of sugar

5 large portobello mushrooms or other large mushrooms

1 red pepper, deseeded and finely sliced lengthways

½ cucumber, peeled in strips, deseeded and cut into chunks

2 large celery stalks, sliced

1½ tablespoons capers, rinsed

4 spring onions, chopped

¼ red onion, sliced lengthways

a handful of flat leaf parsley, a few leaves reserved for serving, the remainder coarsely chopped

2 mozzarella cheeses, 150 g each, torn

sea salt and freshly ground black pepper

caperberries, to serve (optional)

*a baking sheet*

**serves 4**

To make the croutons, tear the bread into large chunks and put onto a baking sheet. Sprinkle with salt and about 2–3 tablespoons of the oil, then cook in a preheated oven at 200°C (400°F) Gas 6 for 10–15 minutes or until golden and crunchy. Remove and cool. (They'll keep for 1–2 days in an airtight container.)

Using a mortar and pestle or a small bowl and the back of a spoon, crush the garlic with 1 teaspoon salt. Add the chilli and crush to form a coarse paste. Add the vinegar and sugar, mix well, then transfer to a large salad bowl. Add about 200 ml of the olive oil and beat well.

Brush the mushrooms with another 2–3 tablespoons of oil, salt and pepper. Heat a stove-top grill pan, add the mushrooms and grill for about 3–4 minutes until barred with brown. Remove and cut into 2 cm slices.

Put the mushrooms into the salad bowl, then add the red pepper, cucumber, celery, capers, spring onions, red onion, parsley and lots of freshly ground black pepper. Toss well, then set aside at room temperature for at least 1 hour, tossing every 20 minutes.

To serve, put the croutons and torn mozzarella into 4 big bowls or deep plates, then pile the mushroom salad mixture on top. Pour over the collected juices from the bowl, add caperberries, if using, and a few herb leaves, then serve.

6 slices fresh white bread, crusts removed and discarded

8 tablespoons fresh pesto

8 large portobello mushrooms, stalks removed

olive oil, for brushing

4 large bunches of cherry tomatoes, on the vine

sea salt and freshly ground black pepper

**to serve**

salad leaves, such as baby spinach or rocket

4 tablespoons extra virgin olive oil

2 tablespoons balsamic vinegar

a handful of basil leaves

**serves 8**

# pesto-stuffed portobello mushrooms
## with roasted vine tomatoes

A great cheat's starter: the pesto is store-bought, the mushrooms make instant containers and the vine tomatoes do their artful bit with almost no prodding or encouragement from you. And the cooking? Kept to minutes. It'll look like you've slaved for hours.

To make the stuffing, put the bread into a food processor and blend to make coarse crumbs. Add the pesto, salt and pepper and blend briefly. Put the mushrooms into a roasting tin, sprinkle with salt and pepper, then brush liberally all over with olive oil. Fill with the pesto stuffing mixture.

Add the vines of cherry tomatoes and sprinkle with salt, pepper and more olive oil. Roast in a preheated oven at 200°C (400°F) Gas 6 for about 8 minutes, or until the tomatoes begin to burst.

To serve, put small bundles of salad leaves on the serving plates and sprinkle with the olive oil and balsamic vinegar. Add a stuffed mushroom and a share of the tomatoes, top with a few basil leaves and serve.

1 kg chestnut mushrooms

10 small shallots, cut into 8 wedges each

2 garlic cloves, crushed

8 sprigs of thyme

125 ml extra virgin olive oil

2 litres chicken or vegetable stock

2 tablespoons crème fraîche

sea salt and freshly ground black pepper

## horseradish cheese

3 cm fresh horseradish root, peeled and very finely grated

½ tablespoon cider vinegar or lemon juice

150 g soft goats' cheese or mascarpone cheese

1 tablespoon crème fraîche

## grissini (optional)

300 g ciabatta bread mix or regular bread mix

plain flour, for dusting

1 tablespoon onion seeds (also known as nigella or kalonji)

*2 large roasting tins*

*a baking sheet, lined with greaseproof paper*

**serves 4**

# roasted chestnut mushroom soup
## with horseradish cheese and grissini

Chestnut mushrooms make this thick, chunky soup unctuously earthy. A spoonful of horseradish cheese added will dress it with creamy spice. You can of course make this soup without the horseradish cheese or the grissini either: they're just delicious optional extras. The soup serves 8 as a starter, 4 as a main course for lunch. It keeps for a few days in the refrigerator.

To make the horseradish cheese, put the horseradish and vinegar into a bowl, then beat in the cheese and crème fraîche. Season with salt and pepper, then chill until needed.

To make the soup, put the mushrooms, shallots, garlic, thyme and olive oil into 2 roasting tins. Sprinkle with salt and pepper, then toss well with your hands. Spread all the ingredients evenly over the pan, with the mushrooms stem upward. Cook in a preheated oven at 190°C (375°F) Gas 5 for about 12 minutes, or until the mushrooms and shallots are just tender.

Transfer the contents of the roasting tins to a large saucepan. Add the stock and bring to the boil on top of the stove. Let simmer for about 5 minutes, then blend in batches in a food processor until smooth but still flecked with little chunks of mushroom. Return to the pan, stir in the crème fraîche and, just before serving, reheat without boiling. Serve in bowls with a spoonful of horseradish cheese on top and the grissini, if using.

**Grissini** Make the bread dough according to the instructions on the packet. After it has doubled in size, knead it briefly, then flour your hands, the work surface and the rolling pin and roll out to 3 mm thick. Slice the dough into 8–10 long sticks about 1½ cm wide, arrange on the prepared baking sheet and leave in a warm place for about 10 minutes, to puff up a little. Put the onion seeds into a bowl, mix in 2 teaspoons water, then spread the mixture over the dough sticks. Bake in a preheated oven at 200°C (400°F) Gas 6 for 8–10 minutes, until lightly browned.

# porcini and root vegetable soup
## with parmesan and parsley

Porcini (also known as ceps or penny buns) are pricey and difficult to buy fresh, but they are widely available dried. They are wonderful for flavouring stocks, soups, braises and sauces – they hold the essence of the pungently scented fresh mushroom. They're best discarded before serving, as their flavour will have been spent in the soup.

10 pieces dried porcini (ceps)

60 g unsalted butter

1 leek, white part only, rinsed and finely chopped

1 bay leaf

a small bunch of flat leaf parsley, tied with kitchen string

4 potatoes, cubed

500 g white root vegetables, such as parsnips or Jerusalem artichokes, thickly sliced

1.5 litres chicken stock

4 tablespoons crème fraîche

4 medium to small fresh porcini or other wild mushrooms, sliced lengthways

sea salt and freshly ground black pepper

**to serve**

freshly shaved Parmesan cheese

truffle oil (optional)

**serves 4**

Put the dried porcini into a cup and cover with warm water. Let soak until very soft, about 20 minutes. Reserve the porcini and their soaking liquid.

Put half the butter into a large saucepan and heat well. Add the leek and bay leaf and fry until softened and translucent. Sprinkle with salt and pepper, then add the parsley, potatoes and root vegetables and cook for 1 minute. Add the stock, the porcini and their soaking liquid, bring to the boil, then reduce the heat and simmer for 20 minutes or until soft.

Discard the bay leaf, parsley and the slices of porcini, then, using a food processor or hand blender, blend to a smooth purée. Stir in the crème fraîche. If the soup is too thick, add a little more stock. Put the remaining butter into a frying pan, heat until foaming, add the sliced mushrooms and fry over high heat until brown on both sides.

When ready to serve, reheat the soup and add salt and pepper to taste. Ladle into bowls and top with the mushrooms, shavings of fresh Parmesan and a sprinkle of truffle oil, if using.

Texture. Flavour. Colour. This Japanese dish has it all. Baby oyster mushrooms are best uncooked – eat them raw to keep their fragile texture, moss-like aroma and subtle colour intact (this is probably what seduced you into buying them in the first place). To toast sesame seeds, put them into a dry frying pan and heat gently, tossing regularly to stop them scorching. When they're flecked golden brown and smell nutty, they're ready.

## pink oyster and shiitake mushrooms
## with crisp tofu and soba noodles

Cut the tofu into 12 small rectangular blocks. Line a plate with 3 sheets of kitchen paper and put the tofu on top to drain for at least 30 minutes. Just before serving, put 1–2 tablespoons of the sunflower oil into a frying pan and heat well. Dust the drained blocks of tofu with the seasoned cornflour, add to the pan and shallow fry on all sides until crisp.

Put 1 litre water into a saucepan and bring to the boil. Stir in the dashi powder, then add the spring onions, 3 tablespoons of the soy sauce and 1 tablespoon of the mirin. Cover with a lid and simmer while you prepare the remaining ingredients.

Put the sesame oil into a frying pan, add the remaining 1 tablespoon sunflower oil and heat gently. Add the shiitake mushrooms and fry until lightly browned all over. Add the remaining soy sauce, mirin and 3 tablespoons of the prepared dashi stock, bring to the boil and reduce until syrupy.

Divide the cooked noodles between 4 preheated bowls, pour over the hot stock (this will reheat the noodles), top with the cooked mushrooms, crisp tofu, fresh oyster mushrooms and toasted sesame seeds, then serve.

300 g block silken tofu

2–3 tablespoons sunflower oil

2 tablespoons cornflour, seasoned with salt

1 sachet instant dashi stock powder

2 spring onions, cut into thirds

6 tablespoons light soy sauce

3 tablespoons mirin (sweetened Japanese rice wine) or dry sherry

1 tablespoon sesame oil

16 shiitake mushrooms, stems trimmed

1 packet soba noodles, cooked *al dente*, according to the instructions on the packet

### to serve

baby pink or yellow oyster mushrooms

1 tablespoon sesame seeds, dry toasted (see recipe introduction)

### serves 4

**pies, tarts and pastries**

# creamy chicken pies
## with portobellos and morels

Fresh morels are available in spring, but can be expensive. Dried morels are available all year round: they are picked and dried in their prime, giving far more flavour than many so-called 'fresh' ones. When rehydrated, they release their smoky-peat flavour and are excellent for turning a chicken pie into something special.

1 cooked chicken, about 1.5 kg

1 onion, halved

2 garlic cloves, sliced

2 bay leaves

2–3 large sprigs of parsley

30 g dried morels, soaked in hot water until soft, about 20 minutes

9 portobello mushrooms

60 g unsalted butter, softened

3 blades of mace or a large pinch of ground mace or grated nutmeg

1 tablespoon plain flour

60 ml double cream

500 g pre-rolled puff pastry, about 1½ packets

1 egg, lightly beaten, to glaze

sea salt and freshly ground black pepper

Dijon mustard, to serve

*4 individual ovenproof bowls or 1 deep pie plate*

**serves 4**

Remove and discard the chicken skin, then shred the meat. To make a stock, put the bones into a saucepan, add the onion, garlic, bay leaves, parsley and 1 litre water. Add salt and pepper and bring to the boil. Reduce the heat and simmer for 20 minutes or until reduced by half. Strain the stock into a bowl and discard the bones and vegetables.

Remove the morels from their soaking liquid and strain the liquid into the stock. Slice 5 of the portobello mushrooms. Put 20 g of the butter into a frying pan, heat until foaming, add the morels and sliced mushrooms and fry until lightly browned. Remove from the pan and reserve.

Add another 20 g butter to the pan, let melt, then stir in the mace (crushed if whole) or nutmeg and the flour and cook for about 1 minute to make a paste. Slowly add the stock, stirring constantly, to form a thick sauce. Add the cream, fried mushrooms and shredded chicken, season well, then heat for 1 minute until simmering.

Put the sheets of pastry onto a work surface and put the bowls upside down on top. Cut around the rims to make 4 discs for the tops of the pies. Spoon the chicken mixture into the bowls. Cover the pies with the pastry discs, lightly press down the edges, then brush all over with the beaten egg. Melt the remaining butter and brush all over the 4 remaining portobello mushrooms. Sprinkle with salt and press one onto each pie. Bake in a preheated oven at 190°C (375°F) Gas 5 for 40 minutes. Remove from the oven and serve with a spoonful of Dijon mustard.

This is where a little bottle of truffle oil will give extra mushroom flavour and a bit of glamour. Mushrooms, especially wild ones, are natural partners with butter, cheese, potato and truffle oil.

## wild mushroom and potato pasties
## with parmesan and truffle oil

Put the potatoes into a saucepan, cover with cold water, bring to the boil and cook until half-done (test with the point of a knife). Drain. Holding the hot potatoes in a cloth, peel off the skins, then cut into thick slices.

Put half the butter into a frying pan, heat until foaming, add the mushrooms, salt and pepper and fry over high heat until beginning to brown on both sides. Add the garlic and herbs, stir-fry for a few seconds, then remove from the heat and let cool.

Put the pastry onto a floured work surface and roll out to about 3 mm thick. Cut into 2 rectangles. Put the potatoes and mushrooms in layers in the middle of each rectangle, sprinkling each layer with truffle oil, shavings of Parmesan, the remaining melted butter, salt and pepper.

Fold in the long edges of the pastry rectangles to contain the filling and make an overlapping join on top. Turn the parcel over and put onto a greased baking sheet. Make 3 parallel diagonal cuts in the tops, brush with the beaten egg, then bake in a preheated oven at 190°C (375°F) Gas 5 oven for about 30 minutes until golden. Cut the parcels diagonally into triangles and serve with salad.

2 large baking potatoes, unpeeled

60 g unsalted butter, melted

4 large fresh porcini, sliced, or 2 handfuls other wild mushrooms or 4 small portobellos, sliced

2 garlic cloves, finely chopped

2 sprigs of thyme or flat leaf parsley, chopped, or 2 teaspoons chopped rosemary leaves

500 g ready-to-roll shortcrust pastry, thawed if frozen

1–2 teaspoons truffle oil

a chunk of Parmesan cheese, shaved

1 egg, lightly beaten, to glaze

sea salt and freshly ground black pepper

salad leaves, to serve

*a baking sheet, greased*

**makes 2: serves 4**

20 g fresh yeast or 1 sachet easy-blend dried yeast*

1 teaspoon honey

500 g strong white bread flour, plus extra for dusting

1 teaspoon salt

oil, for brushing

## mushroom topping

600 g small whole fresh shiitake mushrooms (about 7 per pizza) or mix with other wild varieties

3 tablespoons olive oil

1 tablespoon truffle oil

a handful of small sage leaves

2 garlic cloves, finely chopped or crushed

4 mozzarella cheeses, 150 g each, thinly sliced

sea salt and freshly ground black pepper

*2–3 heavy baking sheets, lined with baking parchment and oiled*

## makes 4 pizzas, 20 cm diameter

*If using easy-blend dried yeast, mix 1 sachet (7 g) with the flour and salt. Stir in the honey and water and proceed with the recipe.*

# sage and shiitake pizza
## with truffle oil

It's tricky to make proper pizza at home. Our ovens can't produce the monstrous amount of heat that's needed to fire them to perfection. However, if you·make the base as thin as possible and avoid putting too much on top – in other words, make an authentic pizza – then it's almost possible. The idea is to get the base just cooked, so it's brittle around the edge yet chewy and soft inside. Use a ready-made pizza base mix if you prefer, and vary the mushroom types too.

To make the pizza base, put 250 ml warm water into a bowl, crumble the fresh yeast over the top, then stir in the honey. Add half the flour and, using your fingers, stir to make a sloppy paste. Cover with a dry tea towel and set aside in a warm place for about 15 minutes. Using your hand again, stir in the salt and remaining flour and work to a smooth dough. Transfer to a floured work surface and knead until silky and soft. Dust with flour, transfer to a clean bowl, cover with a damp cloth and set aside in a warm place for 1 hour or until doubled in size.

Preheat the oven to the highest temperature and put the baking sheets into the oven to heat. Transfer the dough to a floured work surface, punch down, divide into 4 and roll into balls. Heavily dust your work surface with flour, then flatten each ball with a floured rolling pin and, using your fingers (or the rolling pin), stretch into flat long ovals or rounds until very thin. Brush with oil (avoiding the edges).

Put the mushrooms into a bowl, add the olive oil, truffle oil, sage leaves, garlic, salt and pepper and toss well. Arrange the sliced mozzarella over the pizzas, then add the sage leaves and mushrooms, stem side up. Sprinkle with salt and pepper, then transfer to the preheated baking sheets and bake for 8–10 minutes. The time will depend on the heat of the oven. Serve immediately.

This pie carries a double dose of mushrooms, each layer with a different texture and flavour. The one in the picture was devoured immediately, but I think it's better eaten at room temperature. When cool, it will make any picnic go with a swing.

## olive, mushroom and ricotta pie

Put the pastry onto a floured work surface and roll out to about 3 mm thick. Drape it over the rolling pin and unroll over the prepared tart tin. Press gently into the corners and trim, leaving an overhang on the pastry. Knead the scraps back into a ball, roll out again, then cut out a disc slightly larger than the tart tin. Set aside in the refrigerator.

Put half the butter and 1 tablespoon oil into a frying pan and heat until foaming. Add the chopped chestnut mushrooms, garlic, onion, oregano and salt and fry until the onion has softened but not browned. Sprinkle with pepper, stir in the chopped olives, transfer to a bowl and let cool.

Add the remaining butter and oil to the pan, add the portobellos and fry on both sides until browned and soft when pierced with a knife – you may have to work in batches. Sprinkle with salt and pepper and let cool a little.

Put the ricotta and goats' cheese into a bowl, add the nutmeg and mash well. Sprinkle with salt and pepper and mash again. Transfer to the pastry case and spread evenly. Add the portobello mushrooms in a single layer, then spread the mushroom and olive mixture over the top.

Brush the overhanging rim of pastry with beaten egg, then put the reserved disc of pastry on top, very gently pressing the edges together. Trim with a knife, then brush with the beaten egg. Transfer to a baking sheet and bake on the middle shelf of a preheated oven at 180°C (350°F) Gas 4 for 1 hour and 20 minutes, until glossy and golden on top. Sprinkle with the reserved olives and eat warm or at room temperature.

500 g ready-to-roll shortcrust pastry, thawed if frozen

75 g unsalted butter

2 tablespoons olive oil

200 g chestnut mushrooms, chopped

2 garlic cloves, chopped

1 large onion, finely chopped

4 sprigs of oregano, leaves only

80 g black olives, chopped, plus a few whole ones to serve

8 medium portobello mushrooms, stems trimmed

250 g ricotta cheese

100 g goats' cheese

1 teaspoon grated nutmeg

1 egg, lightly beaten, to glaze

sea salt and freshly ground black pepper

*a loose-based tart tin, 24 cm diameter, greased*

*a baking sheet*

**serves 8**

# penny bun quiche

Penny bun is the old-fashioned, more romantic name for what is now known as porcini or cep – I find it just as charming as the Italian porcini, which means 'little pigs'. Call them what you will, they are the kings of the mushroom kingdom: their flavour is rich and intense, steeped with an elixir of mushroominess. Don't make this with dried porcini (they're for flavouring, not eating) – if you don't have any, use other wild or cultivated mushrooms instead.

Put the pastry onto a floured work surface and roll out to about 3 mm thick. Drape over the rolling pin and unroll over the prepared tart tin. Press the pastry into the corners, trim off the excess, prick the base all over with a fork, then chill for 30 minutes until firm. Line the pastry case with baking parchment, fill with rice or baking beans and bake in a preheated oven at 200°C (400°F) Gas 6 for about 10 minutes. Remove from the oven, let cool a little, then remove the paper and beans or rice.

Meanwhile, put half the oil and half the butter into a frying pan, heat until foaming, then add the sliced mushrooms and fry until lightly browned on both sides, gently turning them over once. Remove from the pan and set aside. Add the remaining oil and butter to the pan, heat until foaming, then add the onions, garlic, salt and pepper and fry until the onions have just softened, yet retaining their shape. Meanwhile, put the eggs and cream into a bowl, beat well, then season with salt and pepper.

To assemble the tart, spread half the Fontina over the base, then the cooked sliced potato, sprinkle with salt and pepper, then spread over the remaining cheese. Add the onion mixture, pour over the beaten egg and cream, then arrange the fried sliced mushrooms over the top. Put on a baking sheet and bake in a preheated oven at 180°C (350°F) Gas 4 for 40–45 minutes or until golden and set.

500 g ready-to-roll shortcrust pastry, thawed if frozen

2 tablespoons olive oil

40 g unsalted butter

300 g fresh porcini mushrooms, thickly sliced

2 large Spanish onions, sliced into fine wedges and pulled into petals

3 garlic cloves, finely chopped

3 free range eggs, lightly beaten

225 ml double cream

200 g Fontina cheese, grated

1 very large baking potato, boiled until just tender, peeled and sliced

sea salt and freshly ground black pepper

*a loose-based tart tin, 24 cm diameter, greased*

*baking parchment and rice or baking beans*

**serves 4**

# mushroom brunch pastries

Brunch was invented for people like me: people who stay up too late, get up too late, have missed breakfast but want something like it for lunch (with lunch thrown in too). Somehow the idea of a tart topped with prosciutto and soft poached eggs is so 'brunch' – so simple and good. I also include a vegetarian variation using herbs.

Put the mushrooms onto the baking sheet, sprinkle with salt and pepper, then brush them all over with olive oil – be generous. Cook in a preheated oven at 200°C (400°F) Gas 6 for 8 minutes. Turn the mushrooms over, sprinkle with more olive oil, salt and pepper and roast for a further 5 minutes. Remove from the oven and let cool a little.

Unroll the pastry and trim all the edges (this will help it puff up when it cooks). Cut the pastry in half lengthways and transfer to the baking sheet. Add the mushrooms, stem side up, along the pastry. Using the point of a knife, score a shallow cut in the pastry around each mushroom, so the pastry can rise around them during baking.

Dip the slices of prosciutto in the beaten egg and arrange, slightly ruffled, over the pastry and around the mushrooms. Brush the exposed pastry gaps with plenty of beaten egg. Bake in a preheated oven at 200°C (400°F) Gas 6 for 15–20 minutes until puffed and golden.

To poach the eggs, if using, bring a small saucepan of water to the boil, add the vinegar, reduce to a simmer and swirl the water with a spoon. Crack an egg into a small cup and, close to the surface, slide it into the water. Poach gently for 2 minutes, then carefully transfer to a bowl of warm water, while you cook the remaining eggs. Using a slotted spoon, carefully remove the eggs and dry the bottom of the spoon with kitchen paper. Put an egg on top of each mushroom and cut the pastry into portions. Serve immediately.

**Variation** For the vegetarian alternative on the opposite page, omit the prosciutto and eggs. Dot with sage leaves before baking and serve as above.

6 large portobello mushrooms

olive oil, for brushing

375 g ready-rolled puff pastry, 1 packet, thawed if frozen

12 thin slices prosciutto

1 egg, lightly beaten

6 free range eggs (optional)

4 tablespoons white wine vinegar

sea salt and freshly ground black pepper

*a baking sheet, greased*

**makes 2: serves 8**

What's the secret of a good risotto? It's all in the timing and having an understanding of what you're doing. A risotto can't be rushed. It has to nurtured, tended and fed gently so you end up with a delicious mulch of rice dotted with flavourings. The grains should be tender and fat – but not split – and should have just an edge of bite to them. Never, never wash rice for risotto.

## perfect mushroom risotto

1.5 litres chicken stock

1 tablespoon olive oil

100 g unsalted butter

1 small onion, finely chopped

1 garlic clove, very finely chopped

400 g mushrooms, such as chestnut, small portobello, shiitake or wild mushrooms (but never oyster mushrooms), any large ones sliced

400 g risotto rice, such as carnaroli (the best), vialone nano or arborio

6 pieces dried porcini mushrooms, soaked in 250 ml boiling water for 10 minutes

30 g freshly grated Parmesan cheese, plus extra for serving (optional)

sea salt and freshly ground black pepper

**serves 4**

Put the stock into a saucepan and bring to the boil. Have a ladle ready.

Put the oil and 75 g of the butter into a large, shallow saucepan with a heavy base, then heat until foaming. Add the onion and fry very gently until softened and translucent. Stir occasionally with a wooden spoon. Stir in the garlic, mushrooms, salt and pepper, increase the heat and fry for 1–2 minutes, turning the mushrooms from time to time. Reserve a few mushrooms for serving.

Add the rice and stir gently so the grains are evenly mixed with butter, oil, mushrooms and onion. Strain the porcini soaking water into the pan,* then add just enough boiling stock to cover the grains. Increase the heat to a slow bubble. When the stock has been absorbed to just below the level of the rice, add another ladle. Stir gently from time to time. Repeat until all the stock has been used. After about 18–20 minutes, try the grains: Italians like the heart of the grain to be chalky, but I like mine just a little *al dente*. Do not overcook into a pudding. Remove from the heat, fold in the Parmesan and the remaining 2 tablespoons butter, cover with a lid and, while still quite wet, set aside for a couple of minutes before serving. Serve with extra Parmesan, if using, and the reserved sautéed mushrooms on top.

**\*Note** Discard the porcini after soaking – they have given up all their flavour into the soaking water and have served their purpose.

# mushroom nasi goreng

*Nasi goreng* is an all-day dish in Indonesia. Quite simply, it's fried rice, but you can make it as busy as you like. I find it's a good dish to use up all the delicious pieces left over from the previous day and (usefully) it's best made with day-old rice. Supermarkets now stock many kinds of wild and Asian mushrooms, but if you can't find them you can happily add or subtract ingredients. Try chopped spring onions, chives, coriander and basil, prawn crackers, prawns, cooked meat, hard-boiled eggs, or a stack of stir-fried vegetables. This is a version I make for brunch, but if you don't like eggs, just omit them.

Heat 2 tablespoons of the oil in a wok or large frying pan, add the shallots (reserving some for serving), lemongrass and garlic and fry until the shallots have frazzled at the edges. Add the fish sauce and chopped chillies and fry for 30 seconds. Add the sweet chilli sauce and soy sauce and cook for a further 30 seconds.

Add the mushrooms and rice and stir-fry for about 3 minutes, adding the beansprouts toward the end. Meanwhile, put 2 tablespoons oil in a frying pan, heat well, add the eggs and fry until the whites are set and the yolks still soft.

To serve, divide the rice mixture between warmed serving bowls, sprinkle with the reserved shallot, and top each with a fried egg. Eat with chopsticks.

4 tablespoons peanut or sunflower oil

6 small shallots, sliced lengthways

1 stalk of lemongrass, smashed open but left in one piece

4 garlic cloves, finely sliced

1 tablespoon fish sauce or 1 teaspoon shrimp paste

3 large mild red chillies, deseeded and chopped

1 tablespoons sweet chilli sauce

1 tablespoon dark soy sauce or ½ tablespoon kecap manis*

200 g wild, button, hon shimeji or small shiitake mushrooms

250 g long grain rice, cooked and cooled at least 2 hours before using

a handful of beansprouts

4 free range eggs

**serves 4**

*Available in Asian food stores.

# japanese mushroom sticky rice

1 tablespoon caster sugar

3 tablespoons rice vinegar*

360 g Japanese sushi rice*

3 slices fresh ginger

750 ml chicken stock or water, lightly seasoned with salt

½ sachet instant dashi stock powder*

1 tablespoon sesame oil

1 tablespoon peanut or sunflower oil

20 mushrooms such as chestnut, button, horse or hon shimeji*

2 tablespoons light soy sauce

2 tablespoons mirin (sweetened Japanese rice wine)* or dry sherry

1 tablespoon dried wakame seaweed (optional), soaked in cold water until rehydrated, then drained*

1 bundle of enoki mushrooms (optional)*

1 tablespoon sesame seeds, dry-toasted (see recipe introduction page 25)

**serves 4**

*Available in Asian food stores and large supermarkets.*

A cinch to cook, this dish has all the flavour of sushi. Enoki mushrooms have the tiniest pin-headed caps of all, and are valued for their long, sinuous stems. They have a faint fruity flavour and delicate structure, so don't cook them – eat them just as they are. To prepare, cut off the thick matted base and separate into single stems or clumps, then wrap in clingfilm and keep chilled, otherwise they'll turn brown very quickly. Some of the dry ingredients may sound weird, but most of them can be found in larger supermarkets – dashi is just powdered fish stock and wakame is dried seaweed: add water and they're ready for use.

Put the sugar and rice vinegar into a bowl and stir until dissolved. Set aside.

Wash the the rice in several changes of cold water, then drain thoroughly. Transfer to a medium saucepan, add the ginger and stock, and bring to the boil. Boil for 2 minutes, reduce the heat to the lowest possible, cover the pan with a lid, and simmer very gently for a further 7 minutes. Remove from the heat and let stand for 10 minutes without lifting the lid.

Add the sugar mixture to the saucepan and carefully fold through the rice. Put the dashi powder into a bowl, add 250 ml hot water and dissolve. Set aside. Put the sesame and peanut oils into a frying pan and heat well. Add the 20 mushrooms and fry until lightly browned. Add the soy sauce and mirin and simmer until reduced to a glaze. Add the dashi stock and reduce until syrupy.

To serve, spoon the rice into 4 serving bowls (don't scrape the bottom of the pan). Add the syrupy mushrooms, a share of the wakame seaweed and a few enoki mushrooms (if using), sprinkle with toasted sesame seeds and serve.

This isn't an ordinary baked lasagne: rather, it's a regular pasta dish, using lasagne sheets dressed with layers of rosemary scented porcini under ruckled blankets of soft cheese. No baking. Of course you can use other mushrooms instead of porcini, just don't use dried porcini. Watch out for tunnelling inhabitants in older porcini – if they look suspect, don't buy them, and opt for something else.

# autumn lasagne with soft goats' cheese

30 g unsalted butter

1 tablespoon olive oil

4 very large fresh porcini, or other wild mushrooms or portobellos, sliced

leaves from a sprig of rosemary

16 sheets lasagne, preferably homemade

3 free range egg yolks

3 tablespoons cream

250 g soft, mild goats' cheese or ricotta

shavings of fresh Parmesan cheese

sea salt and freshly ground black pepper

**serves 4**

Put the butter and olive oil into a frying pan and heat until foaming. Add the sliced porcini and rosemary leaves and fry until browned on both sides. Remove from the heat and keep the mushrooms warm.

Bring a large saucepan of salted water to the boil, add the lasagne sheets and cook, stirring gently to keep the sheets separate.

Put the eggs, cream, salt and pepper into a large heatproof bowl set over a saucepan of simmering water. Beat with a metal whisk until the mixture is heated through, about 4 minutes. Drain the lasagne, draping the sheets around the rim of a colander, then add to the bowl of egg mixture and toss carefully. (You have 16 sheets, allowing for breakages.)

To assemble, put a folded sheet of dressed lasagne onto each heated plate. Add a small spoonful of goats' cheese, some shavings of Parmesan and 2 slices of porcini to each serving. Repeat the layers, then top with a sheet of lasagne and extra shavings of Parmesan. Spoon the remaining eggy cream over the top and serve.

# balsamic mushroom spaghetti
## with butternut squash

Bring a very large saucepan of salted water to the boil and add the spaghetti. Cook according to the packet instructions, then drain, reserving a cup of the cooking water. Return the spaghetti to the hot pan and cover with a lid to keep it warm.

Meanwhile, heat the oil in a large frying pan, add the mushrooms and chestnuts and fry on all sides until lightly golden. Add the garlic, sage and butternut squash and fry until lightly browned. Stir in the vinegar and cook until evaporated, then transfer the mushroom mixture to the pan of spaghetti. Add lots of freshly grated Parmesan and some of the reserved cooking water and toss gently. Serve sprinkled with extra Parmesan and lots of freshly ground black pepper.

### Variation:  Herby Mushroom Pasta

Chop a bunch of herbs, such as parsley and thyme, and transfer to a food processor. Cut the crusts off 3 thick slices white bread and crumble the bread into the processor. Process to crumbs. Transfer to a baking sheet, add salt, pepper and 2 tablespoons olive oil. Mix well, then toast in a preheated oven at 110°C (225°F) Gas ¼ for 30 minutes until crisp.

Heat 60 g butter and 2 tablespoons olive oil in a frying pan, add 3 crushed garlic cloves and 4 portobello mushrooms sliced into wedges. Fry for 4–5 minutes until cooked, then add salt and pepper. Toss through the spaghetti as in the main recipe, add half the breadcrumbs and toss again. Serve topped with the remaining breadcrumbs.

400 g spaghetti

2 tablespoons olive oil

300 g chestnut mushrooms and/or large cap wild mushrooms, thickly sliced

10 vacuum-packed peeled chestnuts, sliced lengthways

2 garlic cloves, chopped

a small bunch of sage leaves

350 g peeled and deseeded butternut squash, cut into chunks, then boiled until just tender

½ tablespoon balsamic vinegar

sea salt and freshly ground black pepper

fresh Parmesan, in the block, for grating

**serves 4**

Cultivated shiitake mushrooms are available fresh or dried in Asian stores and supermarkets. Fresh ones have soft, velvety caps and stems with meaty yet delicate flesh, faintly reminiscent of woodsmoke. When cooked, dried shiitakes have a richer aroma and more slippery texture than fresh. If using dried shiitakes, soak for 1 hour in 250 ml cold water, then cut out the tough stems. The liquid can be added to the soup. A flexible main course soup – add or subtract as you like.

## vietnamese duck noodle soup
## with shiitakes and oyster mushrooms

Rub the duck with salt and pepper and put into a sealable plastic bag. Put the five-spice, soy sauce and sugar into a bowl and stir to dissolve the sugar. Add to the bag, seal the bag, then massage the flavour mixture into the duck. Let marinate for 4 hours or overnight in the refrigerator. When ready to cook, transfer to a shallow roasting tin and cook in a preheated oven at 190°C (375°F) Gas 5 for 40 minutes. Either leave whole or cut the meat into chunks.

Meanwhile, to make the soup, put the oil into a deep saucepan, add the shiitakes, fry until just lightly browned, then remove them and reserve.

Add the spareribs, celery, carrots, ginger, dried shrimp, if using, fish sauce and half the spring onions. Add 1.5 litres water and bring to the boil. Reduce the heat and let simmer for about 30 minutes. Strain into a bowl and discard the solids. Return the stock to the rinsed pan, then add salt and pepper to taste.

Add the duck and shiitakes, bring to the boil, reduce the heat and simmer for 5 minutes or until the duck is hot and the mushrooms cooked through.

Finely slice the remaining spring onions. Put the noodles into 4 deep bowls, top with the duck, shiitakes and sliced spring onions, then pour in the very hot stock. Add the oyster mushrooms, crispy shallots, if using, and coriander and serve. Eat with chopsticks, spoons and fingers.

4 duck legs

2 teaspoons Chinese
five-spice powder

3 tablespoons soy sauce

1 tablespoon caster sugar

sea salt and freshly ground
black pepper

## soup

1 tablespoon peanut oil

8 fresh shiitake mushrooms, or
dried ones soaked (see recipe
introduction)

4 pork spareribs, about 500 g,
chopped into 5 cm pieces

2 celery stalks, quartered

2 carrots, thickly sliced

3 cm fresh ginger, peeled and
thickly sliced

1 tablespoon fish sauce

8 spring onions, trimmed

300 g fresh rice noodles*,
or 150 g dried noodles (cooked
according to the packet
instructions and rinsed in cold
water, then drained)

## to serve

baby oyster mushrooms, (optional)

crisp fried salted shallots*

a handful of coriander leaves

## serves 4

*Available in Asian food stores.

A fresh chanterelle or girolle has a delicate aroma of pepper and apricots. With its gold, funnelled cap and long stem, it epitomizes the wild mushroom look – chefs love them. Although available dried, chanterelles are best fresh: if you can't find them, another excellent choice for Asian-inspired dishes is the shiitake.

# seared scallops and mushrooms
## with fluffy jasmine rice

Put 1 tablespoon of the oil into a wok and heat well. Add the shallots and celery stalks and stir-fry until they begin to brown. Add the garlic and Thai green curry paste and stir-fry until the paste changes colour.

Stir in the sugar, fish sauce, lime juice and mushrooms, then add the chicken stock and bring to the boil for about 5 minutes, until reduced by half.

Meanwhile, put the remaining oil into a frying pan and heat until smoking. Sprinkle the scallops with salt, add to the pan and sear for about 30 seconds on each side.

Add the celery leaves and curry paste mixture to the frying pan and bring to the boil for no more than 1 minute, or the scallops will become tough and rubbery. Top with basil, if using, and serve with steamed jasmine rice.

*Steamed rice What the Chinese call 'steamed rice' is really boiled-steamed. Everyone has a favourite way of cooking rice, but I prefer the Asian way. Put washed rice into a saucepan and cover with enough water to come one finger's joint above the rice. Bring to the boil for 2 minutes, cover tightly with a lid, reduce the heat to very low and cook for 8 minutes without lifting the lid. Turn off the heat and, again without lifting the lid, set aside for 10 minutes. You will have perfect fluffy rice.

3 tablespoons peanut oil

3 small shallots, chopped

2 celery stalks, with leaves, stems chopped, leaves kept whole

2 garlic cloves, chopped

2 teaspoons Thai green curry paste

1 tablespoon muscovado sugar

1 tablespoon fish sauce

freshly squeezed juice of 1 lime

200 g chanterelle or shiitake mushrooms

200 ml chicken stock

12 large scallops, trimmed

sea salt

**to serve**

basil leaves (optional)

steamed jasmine rice*

**serves 4**

4 small sea bass fillets, halved

½ tablespoon sesame oil

4 large garlic cloves, sliced lengthways

3 cm fresh ginger, peeled and thickly sliced

1 mild red chilli, deseeded and sliced

8 small onions, halved lengthways

8 baby bok choy or 4 regular

1 tablespoon cornflour mixed with 2 tablespoons cold water

1 tablespoon soy sauce

8 medium oyster mushrooms

a handful of Chinese dried black fungus, soaked in warm water

sea salt and freshly ground black pepper

steamed rice (page 50), to serve

peanut or sunflower oil, for deep-frying

**batter**

100 g plain flour

½ teaspoon salt

1 teaspoon baking powder

125 ml beer

2 tablespoons sunflower oil

2 egg whites

*4 small clay pots or small ovenproof dishes*

**serves 4**

Chinese dried black fungus is available in Asian food stores. Soak it in warm water for 30 minutes before using – the pieces will bloom into beautiful shapes, and are usually very large. Cut out any hard stems or spots before adding to the dish. This two-stage method of clay-pot cooking is a typical Chinese technique – if you don't have any clay pots, use other small ovenproof dishes.

# chinese hotpot of sea bass
## with black fungus and mushrooms

To make the batter, put the flour, salt, baking powder, beer and oil into a bowl and mix well. Set aside for 30 minutes.

Put the egg whites into a second bowl and whisk to soft peak stage. Just before you are ready to fry the fish, fold the egg whites into the batter. Fill a wok or deep-fryer one-third full with oil and heat to 190°C (375°F) or until a cube of bread will brown in 30 seconds. Working in batches, dip each piece of fish into the batter, then immediately into the hot oil and fry until crisp and golden. Remove with a meshed or slotted spoon and drain on kitchen paper.

Pour off all except 1 tablespoon of the oil, add the sesame oil, garlic and ginger and stir-fry until just starting to brown. Add the chilli, onions, salt and pepper and stir-fry briefly.

Add 200 ml water, bring to the boil and reduce until the onions are almost tender. Add the bok choy, let soften for about 30 seconds, then add the cornflour and water mixture and soy sauce. Heat until simmering, then add a further 400 ml water to make a sauce. Add the oyster mushrooms and the drained black fungus, stir through and heat until simmering.

Divide the wok mixture between 4 clay pots or dishes. Tuck 2 pieces of fish into each pot. Cook, uncovered, in a preheated oven at 220°C (425°F) Gas 7 for 5 minutes to heat through, then serve with steamed rice.

The mild flavour and chunky meatiness of cod suits the strong presence of fried wild mushrooms. You can also add crispy fried bacon lardons to the mushroom mixture for a little salty crunch. Use any wild mushrooms – supermarkets sell many cultivated so-called 'wild' varieties, so we don't all have to go hunting for our own.

# buttered mushroom greens
## with pan-roasted cod

Put the cod onto a plate or board and sprinkle with salt and pepper on both sides. Set aside for about 30 minutes – the salt will help firm up the texture and improve the flavour.

Put the potatoes into a large saucepan, cover with cold water, bring to the boil, add a pinch of salt and cook until tender, about 20 minutes. Drain and return to the hot pan, let steam dry for a few minutes, then add enough butter and milk to make a smooth mash. Mash well, then sprinkle with truffle oil and mash again. Cover and keep hot.

Meanwhile, bring another large saucepan of salted water to the boil, add the greens and blanch for 1½ minutes. Drain and plunge into cold water, then drain again. Put the 60 g butter into a wide saucepan, heat until foaming, add the shallots and garlic and cook until softened. Add the mushrooms, fry for a further 2 minutes, then add the beer and simmer until reduced by half. When almost ready to serve, stir in the greens and keep the mixture warm.

To cook the fish, put the olive oil and the 40 g butter into a large frying pan and heat until foaming. Add the cod, skin side down, and fry for about 3 minutes – don't move it about in the pan. Carefully slide a spatula under each fillet and turn it over. Fry on the flesh side for about 2–3 minutes more or until just done (when the flesh is opaque in the centre).

Serve on preheated plates with the truffled mash and buttered mushroom greens, pour over any collected buttery juices from the mushroom pan, then sprinkle with a few drops of truffle oil.

4 thick slices of cod fillet

3 tablespoons olive oil

40 g unsalted butter

sea salt and freshly ground black pepper

### truffled mash

1 kg large floury potatoes, halved

a pinch of salt

unsalted butter, for mashing

about 100 ml full-cream milk

1½ teaspoons truffle oil, plus extra to serve

### mushroom greens

12 large leaves of cabbage, cut in half and ribs removed

60 g unsalted butter

3 shallots, finely chopped

2 garlic cloves, chopped

500 g wild mushrooms (any selection)

100 ml beer

### serves 4

# oyster mushroom and prawn gumbo
## with sausage and bacon

16 uncooked tiger prawns,
shell on

3 tablespoons olive oil

12 oyster mushrooms

1/2 teaspoon salt

1/4 teaspoon cayenne pepper

2 teaspoons paprika

freshly crushed black pepper

4 tablespoons plain flour

100 g unsalted butter

3 onions, chopped

4 celery stalks, chopped

2 red or orange peppers,
deseeded and coarsely chopped

4 sprigs of thyme

4 fat garlic cloves, chopped

250 ml chicken stock

2 cured spicy pork sausages,
chopped

a handful of black trompette
mushrooms (optional)

a handful of fresh flat leaf parsley,
chopped, plus leaves to serve

2 slices smoked bacon,
cooked until crisp

boiled rice, to serve

**serves 4**

Gumbo is a lightly spiced Creole stew from Louisiana—a hotch-potch of seafood and meat traditionally thickened with a well browned roux (a mixture of flour and fat) and filé powder or chopped okra. It's an adaptable recipe, using whatever is at hand. I've used black trompette and oyster mushrooms, but choose varieties available locally.

Put 1 litre water into a large saucepan and bring to the boil. Add the prawns and cook for about 2 minutes. Strain, keeping their cooking water.

Peel the prawns and put the shells into a food processor. Process until just chunky, then transfer to the pan and add 2 tablespoons of the olive oil. Sear over high heat until browned and aromatic. Add the reserved cooking water and simmer, part-covered with a lid, for 30 minutes, to make a stock. Strain and discard the residue: you should have about 500 ml.

Put the oyster mushrooms into a bowl with the salt, cayenne, paprika, pepper and 2 tablespoons of the flour. Toss well. Put 30 g of the butter into a frying pan, add the remaining 1 tablespoon oil and heat well. Add the floured mushrooms and fry until just brown. Transfer to a bowl. Wipe the pan clean with kitchen paper, then add a further 30 g of the butter, heat well, then add the vegetables, thyme and garlic and fry until softened.

Sprinkle the remaining flour over the vegetables, add the remaining butter, then cook, stirring frequently to prevent burning, until the vegetables are browned. Transfer to a large saucepan.

Put the saucepan over medium heat, then slowly, stirring gently, add the chicken stock, then enough prawn stock to make a thickish sauce. Add the sausage and the trompette mushrooms, if using. Reduce the heat to low, part-cover with a lid and simmer for 20 minutes, stirring and scraping the pan to prevent it catching. Stir in the cooked prawns and parsley 2–3 minutes before serving. Add salt and pepper, put the bacon on top and serve with rice.

# portobellos braised in red wine
## with thyme polenta

This is cold weather food and portobellos, being meaty fellows, are the fungi that fit the bill. If you like meat, but sometimes share your table with a vegetarian, this dish has all the heartiness of something you'd expect to find made with beef.

Put 3 tablespoons of the oil into a very large frying pan, heat well, then add the mushrooms and fry at a high heat on both sides until brown. They sop up a lot of oil, so don't give them too much: they'll be cooked properly later. Remove from the pan, cover and set aside.

Add half the butter and the remaining 1 tablespoon olive oil to the pan, heat well, then add the onion, celery, carrots, garlic, bay leaves, salt and pepper and fry until all are lightly caramelized. Add the vinegar, boil until almost dry, then repeat with the Madeira. Stir in the tomato purée, wine and stock, bring to the boil, then simmer for 30 minutes or until reduced by two-thirds or enough to allow the mushrooms to return to the pan without being swamped.

Return the mushrooms to the pan, pushing them into the gravy stem side up. Season with salt and pepper, cover and simmer very gently for 12 minutes.

Cook the polenta according to the packet instructions, adding the thyme leaves to the cooking water. Stir in the Parmesan and remaining butter. Transfer to serving bowls and, using the spoon, press a deep well in the centre of each. Spoon the gravy and vegetables into the wells, top with the braised mushrooms and serve.

4 tablespoons olive oil

4 very large portobello mushrooms

60 g unsalted butter

1 large onion, finely chopped

2 celery stalks, finely chopped

2 carrots, finely chopped

3 garlic cloves, finely chopped

3 bay leaves

2 tablespoons sherry vinegar or red wine vinegar

125 ml Madeira or port

2 teaspoons tomato purée

400 ml red wine

500 ml chicken or vegetable stock

250 g 'instant' polenta

4 sprigs of thyme, leaves only

50 g freshly grated Parmesan cheese

sea salt and freshly ground black pepper

**serves 4**

A few slices of dried porcini bubbled with stock will work some wild mushroom magic into any rich gravy. Always keep a packet or two of dried porcini in an airtight container in a cool, dark cupboard, and you'll always have some instant wild mushroominess available.

20 g dried porcini mushrooms

1 tablespoon sunflower oil

40 g unsalted butter

1 large onion, chopped

3 garlic cloves, finely chopped

3 tablespoons sherry vinegar

100 ml Madeira or sherry

750 ml chicken stock

350 g mushrooms, preferably wild

1 tablespoons cornflour mixed with 2 tablespoons cold water

sea salt and freshly ground black pepper

mashed potatoes, to serve

**peppered roast pork**

2 racks of pork (8 ribs), frenched and chined by the butcher

olive oil

2 large whole bulbs of garlic, separated into cloves but unpeeled

sea salt and 2 tablespoons cracked black peppercorns

**serves 4**

# peppered roast pork
## with mushroom gravy and mash

Put the porcini into a bowl, cover with 125 ml hot water and soak until soft.

Put the sunflower oil and half the butter into a frying pan, heat until foaming, then add the onion and half the chopped garlic and fry until softened and translucent. Add salt, pepper and vinegar, bring to the boil and simmer until almost dry. Add the Madeira, stock and the porcini with their soaking water, bring to the boil and simmer for 20 minutes until reduced by half. Strain into a bowl.

Meanwhile, put the pork into a roasting tin, flesh side up, and rub well with salt and pat on the pepper. Brush with olive oil, tuck the whole garlic cloves underneath and roast in a preheated oven at 220°C (425°F) Gas 7 for 25 minutes. Reduce the temperature to 190°C (375°F) Gas 5 and roast for a further 25 minutes (if you have a fan-assisted oven, reduce these temperatures by 10°C). Remove from the oven, cover with foil and let rest for about 10 minutes or so before slicing into chops.

When the pork is ready, put the remaining butter into the frying pan, heat well, add salt and pepper, the mushrooms and remaining chopped garlic and fry for about 2 minutes until golden brown. Reheat the gravy and strain into the mushroom frying pan. Add the cornflour and water mixture and let simmer for a few minutes to make a thick gravy.

Spoon hot mashed potatoes into 4 deep bowls, add the pork chops and mushroom gravy and serve.

In Turkey, they make fantastic lamb dishes – this recipe is based on the flavours I found there. I made it with local hedgehog mushrooms, but you can use any meaty wild mushroom you have available, or the brown chestnut – the more flavourful kind of cultivated mushroom.

about 1 kg trimmed lamb shoulder meat, cut into bite-sized chunks

150 g chestnut mushrooms or large wild mushrooms, about 12

1 teaspoon ground allspice

2 teaspoons ground cumin

1 large onion, quartered

2 garlic cloves

3 tablespoons olive oil, plus extra for brushing

a small handful of mint leaves, coarsely chopped

a small handful of marjoram, coarsely chopped

1 tablespoon raisins

200 ml meat stock, preferably lamb

3 baking potatoes, peeled and finely sliced

sea salt and freshly ground black pepper

**serves 4**

# turkish lamb and mushroom hotpot
## with potato crust

Put the lamb into a large casserole dish, add the mushrooms, allspice, cumin and pepper and toss well. Put the onion and garlic into a food processor and work to a coarse purée. Stir into the lamb and set aside to marinate for 1 hour.

Stir in the salt and olive oil and put on top of the stove over a high heat. Fry the lamb for about 3 minutes until the spices smell aromatic.

Add the mint, marjoram, raisins and stock, stir well and bring to the boil. Reduce the heat to low, cover with a lid and simmer gently on top of the stove for about 1 hour.

Remove the lid and cover the meat and mushrooms with an overlapping layer of sliced potatoes. Sprinkle with salt and pepper and brush all over with oil. Cook in a preheated oven at 190°C (375°F) Gas 5 for 1 hour, 10 minutes. Alternatively, divide the meat mixture between 4 individual ovenproof dishes, cover with potato and cook as before.

# index